A Perfect 10

10 Piano Solos in 10 Styles

Melody Bober

What could be more exhilarating than receiving the score of a perfect "10"? Olympic athletes, as well as competitors in sports, dance, and music, strive for those high marks. In fact, we all work to achieve perfection in the activities we enjoy. Wouldn't it be wonderful to find a resource that offers pianists a chance to shine at any level—solos in all styles and from all periods of music history that promote technical skills and offer the dream to succeed in performance?

Introducing *A Perfect 10*, Book 1, a collection of solos designed to promote musical excellence for the elementary to late-elementary pianist. I chose a favorite teaching piece from the four stylistic periods—Baroque, Classical, Romantic, and Contemporary. I then wrote six original pieces in jazz, blues, ragtime, Latin, ballad, and showstopper styles. Many of these pieces have optional duet accompaniments. These 10 solos provide students with technical challenges as well as expressive opportunities for musical growth in mood, rhythm, melody, harmony, form, articulation, and dynamics.

You do not have to be an Olympic hopeful to achieve a perfect "10," but you might feel like one as you practice and perform these selections!

Best wishes for successful music making,

Melody Bober

Contents

Blue Shoes Blues 6

Dance 19

Evening in Spain 2

Got Those Monday Blues 10

Ragtime Fun 8

Springtime 16

Study 18

Trampoline Tricks 12

Two Marches

   I 14

   II 15

Wishing Well Waltz 4

Copyright © 2013 by Alfred Music
All rights reserved.
ISBN-10: 0-7390-9840-3
ISBN-13: 978-7390-9840-0

Evening in Spain

Latin

Melody Bober

DUET ACCOMPANIMENT: Student plays one octave higher.

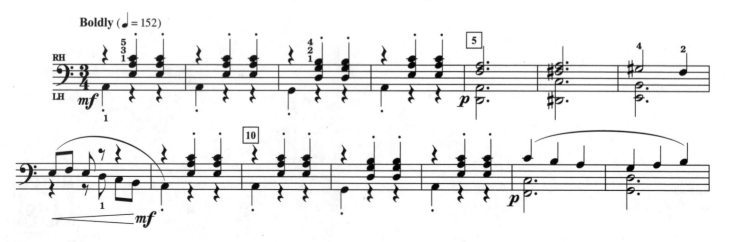

Wishing Well Waltz

Ballad

Melody Bober

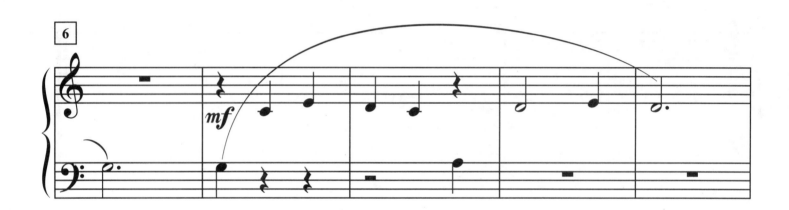

DUET ACCOMPANIMENT: Student plays one octave higher.

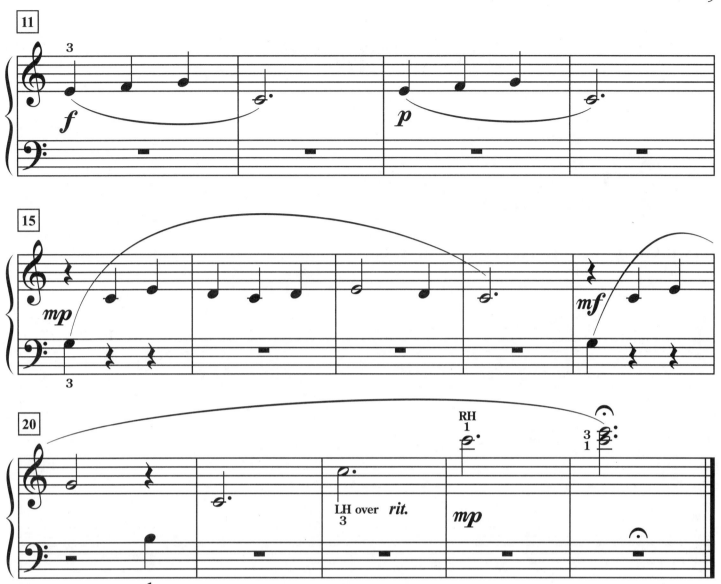

Blue Shoes Boogie

Jazz

Melody Bober

DUET ACCOMPANIMENT: Student plays one octave higher.

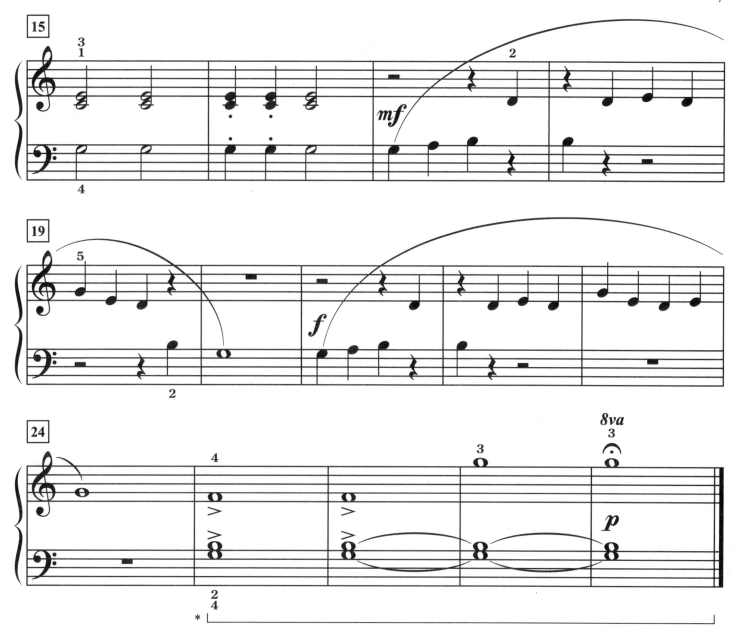

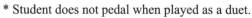

* Student does not pedal when played as a duet.

Ragtime Fun

Ragtime

Melody Bober

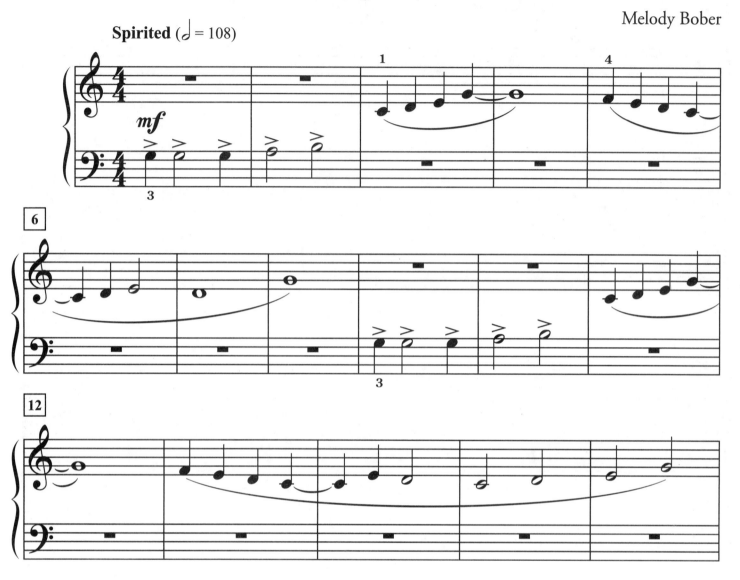

DUET ACCOMPANIMENT: Student plays one octave higher.

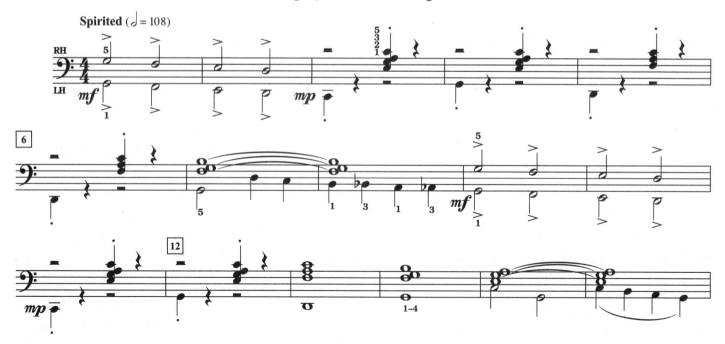

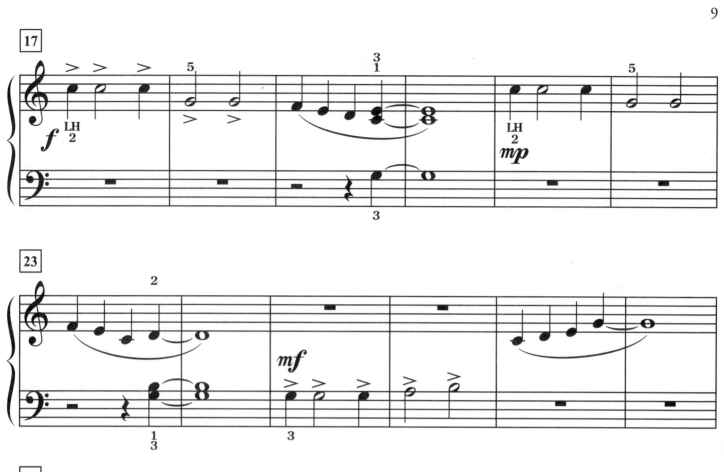

Got Those Monday Blues

Blues

Melody Bober

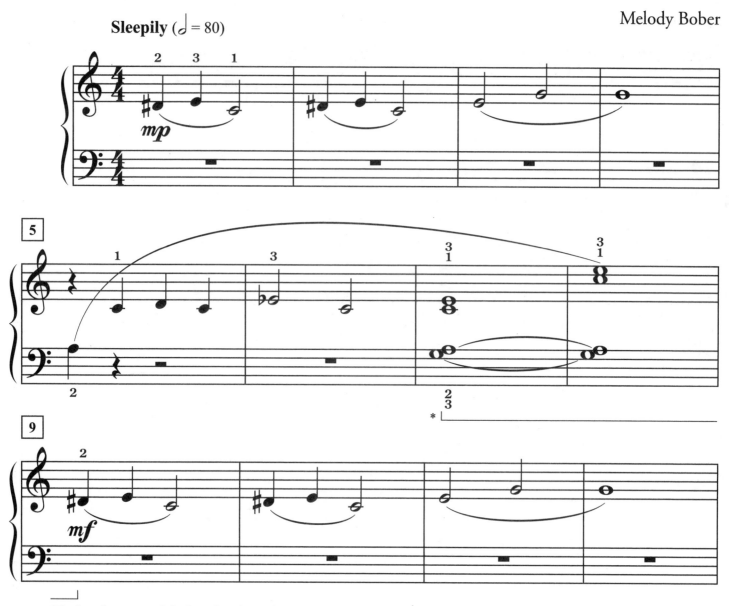

*Student does not pedal when played as a duet.

DUET ACCOMPANIMENT: Student plays one octave higher.

Trampoline Tricks

Showstopper

Melody Bober

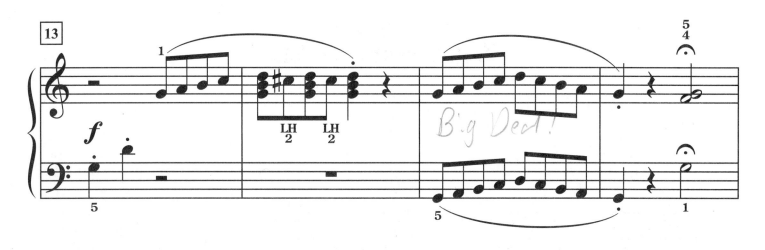

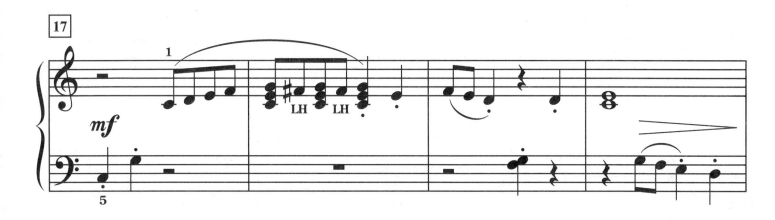

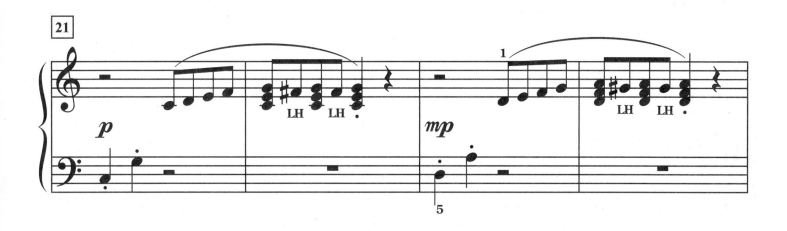

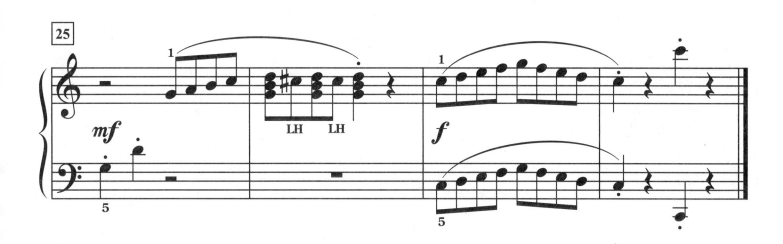

Two Marches

Classical

I.

Daniel Gottlob Türk
(1756–1813)

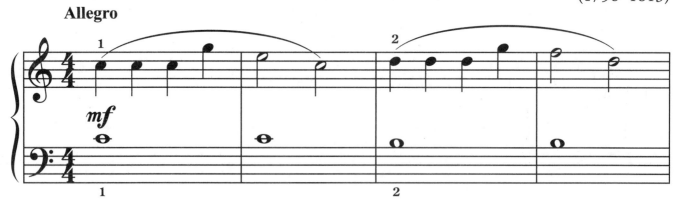

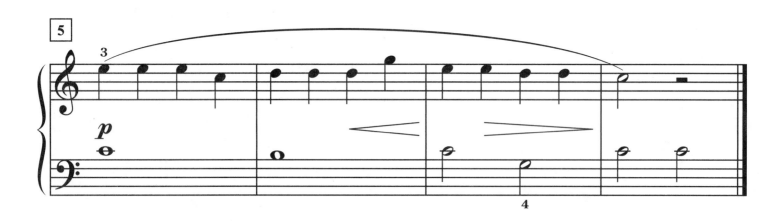

DUET ACCOMPANIMENT: Student plays one octave higher.

Melody Bober

II.

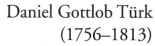

Daniel Gottlob Türk
(1756–1813)

Allegro

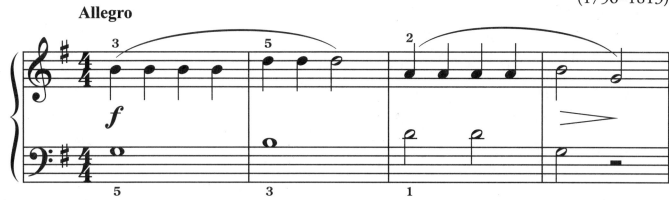

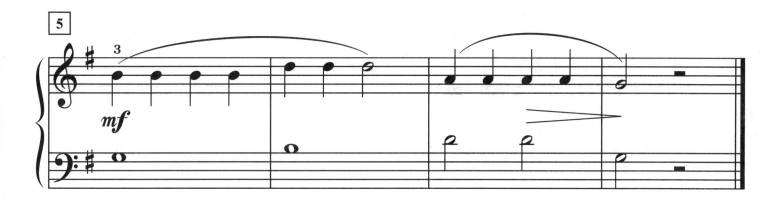

DUET ACCOMPANIMENT: Student plays one octave lower.

Melody Bober

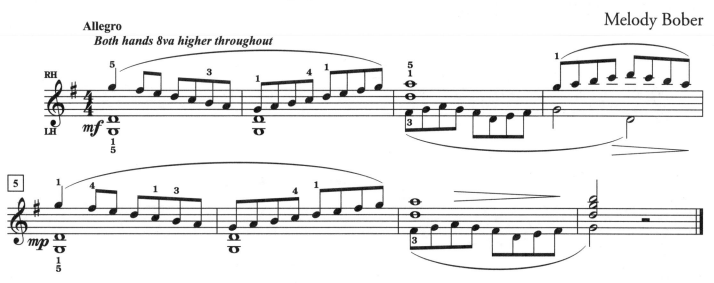

Springtime

Romantic

Cornelius Gurlitt (1820–1901)
Op. 117, No. 5

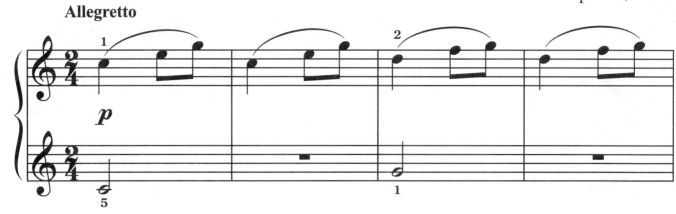

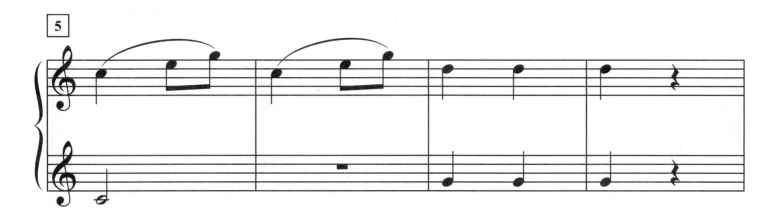

DUET ACCOMPANIMENT: Student plays one octave higher.

Melody Bober

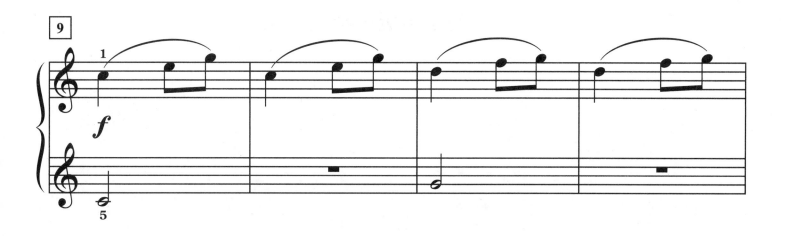

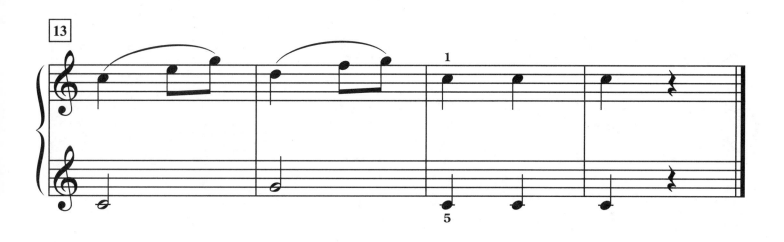

Study
(The First Term at the Piano)

Contemporary

Béla Bartók
(1881–1945)

DUET ACCOMPANIMENT: Student plays one octave higher.

Melody Bober

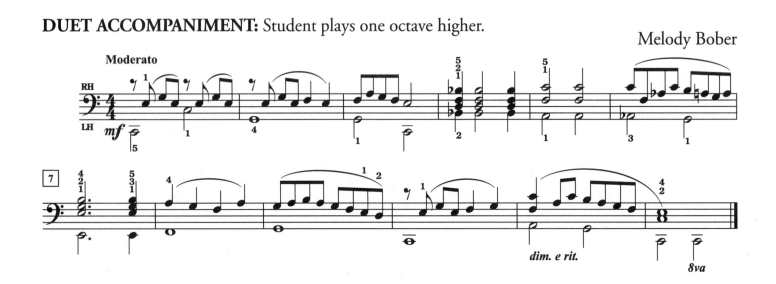

Dance

Baroque

Joachim van der Hofe
(c. 1612)

DUET ACCOMPANIMENT: Student plays as written.

Melody Bober